The Secret Blueprint to More (_____*)

* You fill in the blank

Make more money, increase your success, be happier, create a better life and dominate your market by eliminating your barriers to success and mastering your mindset.

_____

Chris M. Sprague

Sangnite, LLC
Collegeville, PA

The Secret Blueprint to More (_____*)

Copyright © 2012 Chris M. Sprague

This book includes numerous links to websites. If you find anything wrong with any of them, please email bookissue@sangnite.com.

Disclaimer to reader: Your goal is to increase your success. The goal of this book is to help you change your mindset and increase your success. There is no suggestion, endorsement or implication you should do anything illegal, immoral or unethical. In the end, you are responsible for your actions and for whether or not you chose to take this advice.

ISBN-13: 978-0615747309
ISBN-10: 0615747302

Sangnite, LLC
Collegeville, PA

Dedication

This book is dedicated to my beloved wife Kristin for sticking by me all these years. Without her love and support, this book would not have been possible.

Contents

Foreword

"Chris M. Sprague delivers timeless wisdom and proven strategies in a clear, step-by-step blueprint. A cut-to-the-chase, resource any business owner will turn to again and again. Through personal growth and self-discovery, business success CAN be yours! Packed with street smarts and practical tips on how to "run the race", *The Secret Blueprint to More (_____*)* leads you through exercises that will uncover key hidden barriers and empower you to ACHIEVE.

Praise for Sprague! He's simplified mastering your mindset so you can master your world."

To your success!

Charlie McDermott
Founder and CEO

The Business &
Entrepreneur Network
www.BENresults.com

Preface

Whether you know it or not, you have one or more barriers or obstacles to the life you have always dreamed of and to epic success. If you are one of the millions of people who do not realize these obstacles and barriers exist and only see the end result of the barriers (for example, your business is not succeeding at the level you want) that is ok, for now. Many people who consider themselves successful have no idea that they could increase their profits 100%, 200% or even 500% by eliminating their unseen barriers.

The key to breaking through and eliminating these barriers is for you to master your mindset. In some cases, this involves being 100% comfortable with the way you are thinking and in other cases, it involves transforming your mindset. Because, when you change the way you think about things, the things you think about change. In this book, you will learn how to master your mindset and break through both seen and unseen barriers by first learning the key hidden barriers to more (_____*) and then being empowered to think differently.

Right now, you may be thinking, "Forget about the hidden barriers, it is the ones I already know about that need to be fixed." I agree that the visible barriers need to be resolved. However, most of them are a direct result of hidden barriers and without eliminating the hidden barriers you might as well be beating your head against a brick wall.

Start your journey… now!

The Secret Blueprint to More (_____*)

Introduction

This book is divided into 2 sections. Section 1 will empower you to discover the Hidden Barriers to More (_____*) and unlock the keys to overcoming them. The nine key hidden barriers to more (_____*) are:

- ✓ Being Incongruent / Incongruous
- ✓ Anticipating the Result
- ✓ Giving an Overly Explanatory Explanation
- ✓ Using the Dreaded 'ly' Words
- ✓ Trying to Get Married Before Dating
- ✓ Focusing on You and not Your Clients
- ✓ Using up All Your Energy on *Busy Work*
- ✓ Your Timing is Off
- ✓ Chasing the Money and not Your Passion

Section 2 will empower you by unlocking the secrets of successful thinking and show you how to transform your mindset by covering the following topics.

- ✓ Understand your Strengths and Weaknesses
- ✓ Do it Twice with a purpose
- ✓ Create the Right Inner Circles
- ✓ Record Your Thoughts
- ✓ Flip Things Around
- ✓ Try Something New
- ✓ Reflect and Plan

Section #1: Discover the Hidden Barriers to More (_____*) and Unlock the Keys to Overcoming them

> *"Only when you uncover your hidden barriers to success, can you truly live the life you want to live and co-create the success you deserve." Chris M. Sprague*

Hidden Barrier to More (_____*) #1:
Being Incongruent / Incongruous

What does it mean to be incongruent or incongruous?

Incongruent means something that is not compatible with what is correct while incongruous means inconsistent or not harmonious in character. While either one is fine, for our purposes we will go with incongruous. That is unless I keep screwing up and using incongruent because I have used it for so long (smile).

Here is the challenge about being incongruous. Most people are doing it without realizing it. At one time or another, many people say one thing while their subconscious is thinking another. This should not be confused with being two-faced. Being two-faced is where you are consciously thinking one thing and saying another. What we are talking about here goes much deeper.

When you are subconsciously incongruous, your body gives off signals that betray you. Experts refer to these signals as micro-expressions. Before we go further into micro-expressions, we will look at a case study of a client who was being incongruous.

4 The Secret Blueprint to More (_____*)

Case Study: The Relationship Marketer

I work with many network marketers, relationship marketers and multi-level marketers. One of these clients, we will call him Michael (not his real name) specializes in multi-level marketing. We have all heard the comments and perceptions about many multi-level marketers. Some of these comments and perceptions include:

> *The companies they represent scam people.*
>
> *Their representatives beg and bug their family and friends to join.*
>
> *They are always trying to get everyone they meet to join.*
>
> *The only people who make money are the first ones in.*

While there are other assumptions about businesses like this and the people who participate in them, the other assumptions are not critical to this discussion.

When we talked about Michael's business, he proceeded to cross his arms, lean back and stumble through his answer. This immediately conveyed a lack of confidence in the business he was representing. We began to discuss this apparent lack of confidence and he immediately became defensive, began to argue and say that he was confident. The rest of our session focused on coaching him though why he appeared to lack confidence.

Think about it, if he answered everybody else the same way he answered me, how many other people thought the same thing (consciously or subconsciously) and would not give him the time of day to even listen to what he had to say. Some of you are probably thinking, "That's fine, but you know what to look for and we don't." If that is you, wonderful! You are partially right. Everyone has a subconscious that knows what to look for, even if the conscious mind is not aware of it.

From the time of our ancestors, we have been bred to recognize certain *micro-expressions*. These may come in the form of a face-twitch, crossed arms, a furrowed brow and in more extreme cases bared teeth. To our ancestors, telling whether or not they were in danger within a split-second was the difference between being alive or dead. Hence, learning to sense danger and automatically activate their fight-or-flight response was an absolute necessity to their survival. Think of it this way. There are book smarts and then there are street smarts.

Did you ever wonder what street smarts are?

Street Smarts are the fine-tuned response to micro-expressions that some people have. Think about it.

6   The Secret Blueprint to More (_____*)

*Why are some of the most successful people (like Richard
Branson and Bill Gates) people who drop out of school?*

It is because they need to read people to survive or learn
to read people to thrive and instinctively know what to do in
almost every situation. They have street smarts.

These are the things that most schools do not teach you.
School is great for many people and it does teach people
some of the skills they need to survive. However, there is so
much more out there. By now you are probably saying,
"This is great. Get to breaking through the barrier of being
incongruous already!" Alright, here we go!

The best way to break through the barrier of being
incongruous is to do the following.

Understand and Accept Who You Are

Overcoming Barrier #1:
Understand and Accept Yourself

The question many people ask is this. "How do you overcome being incongruous?" In simplest terms, you need to understand yourself, accept who you are and accept your strengths and weaknesses. Many people think they know who they are. Many people also think they know how others see them. Ask yourself these questions:

Do you really know who you are?

Do you really know how others see you?

How can you find out the answers to these two key questions?

While there are many personality and strengths-based assessments out there, the two assessments I have found to be highly successful are StrengthsFinder 2.0® (see note 1) and StandOut® (see note 2). What follows is my description, impressions and opinions of both StrengthsFinder 2.0® and StandOut® along with personal stories to illustrate the changes these books and assessments have made in my life.

8   The Secret Blueprint to More (_____*)

Once you get the chance to use these books and assessments, share your story by visiting this site.

http://TheSecretBlueprintToMore.com/accept

Method #1: StrengthsFinder 2.0®

StrengthsFinder 2.0® is both a book and an assessment test. Its questions are designed to help you understand yourself better and objectively determine your true strengths. Taking this assessment will either validate the strengths you believe you have or open your eyes to strengths you do not know you have. One of the key points of StrengthsFinder 2.0® is that your mood or state-of-mind is not supposed to play a major role in the results. However, from taking the assessment multiple times it appears who you are *being* during the assessment affects the results in a minor way. Given this, I recommend you taking the assessment twice, at least three months apart. This will do two things for you.

First, it will show you how you are growing and changing. If you are like many of my clients, you will see a few minor differences between the first and second assessment.

Second, it will allow you to understand much better how people view you when you are *being* a certain way. If your results are completely different between the first and second assessment, you will understand that people view you differently depending on who you are being on a daily basis. While this may make sense to most people, it is an eye-opener for others. When I first took the assessment, here were the results:

Restorative, Achiever, Individualization, Strategic and Ideation

After taking the assessment again a year later, here were the results:

Futuristic, Connectedness, Input, Strategic and Ideation

We will firs focus on the three areas that were different. The results of the first the assessment revealed someone who likes to improve themselves (restorative), someone who likes to produce quality results (achiever) and someone who gains insights from their mistakes and does better the next time (individualization). What is very interesting about these results is the situation I was in before I took the assessment. I was laid off for over a year, working to improve myself to get another job, working hard to produce quality results in my job search and talking to prospective employers about how I would do things for them.

10 The Secret Blueprint to More (_____*)

The results of the second assessment revealed someone who is inspired by what the future holds (futuristic), someone who believes that everything happens for a reason (connectedness) and someone who loves to learn and craves to know more (input). Before this assessment, the business was growing thanks to the connections made over the past year and each day the future was looking brighter and brighter.

As you can see, I was in a different place before each assessment and the results were different. However, two things did not change, strategic and ideation. This shows someone who is always looking for ways to get things done (strategic) and is fascinated by ideas (ideation). Once I turned the 2-book project of another author into a 36-book project and was dubbed *The Big Idea Guy,* so these two strengths make perfect sense. It also makes sense that who I was being did not affect these two strengths. Because, regardless of whom I am being, creative alternatives to issues and always getting charged up by the thought of coming up with new ideas are the best part of the creative process. Here is another situation from the past that these assessments brought to light.

I was managing a group of Business Intelligence professionals. After work, the time that should have been spent sleeping was spent renovating the house. On a regular basis, *bedtime* would be 3, 4 or 5 am. Sleep would come only after the remodeling was done. It was a fun distraction from the daily grind of the job. The usual day would be; work 12 hours, spend some time with family, remodel the house for 5+ hours, get an hour or two of sleep and head into work. After doing this for 6 months or so, the remodeling was finally finished.

A few weeks later, one of the team members said that the team was glad the remodeling was over because the team could tell the nights the remodeling was happening. They said they could tell because I was in a different mood and treated the team differently after those nights.

This was a shock! At that time, I was not in-tune with myself enough to understand that I was being different at work after nights when the remodeling was happening. I just thought I was tired and that nobody noticed. Had an assessment like this been taken back then, maybe it would have saved the team a whole bunch of stress and frustration.

At the time this book was written, I was not an affiliate for the producers of the StrengthsFinder 2.0® assessment. However, The BE A Success Academy, which we will review later, goes into much more detail on this and other assessments.

Method #2: StandOut®

StandOut® is also a book and an assessment test. The assessment is meant to tell you what your two best roles in an organization would be based on what you would do in certain situations. The results are not affected by your preconceived notions about what roles would be best for you or what your skills are. In other words, the assessment tells you what makes you stand out.

I first heard about this assessment at the 2012 Chick-fil-A Leadercast® event. At the event, the author of the book, Marcus Buckingham, was a featured speaker. He gave a brief overview of the book and assessment. As he went through the roles, he got to the *Influencer* role. He described an Influencer as someone who considered every conversation a close. Immediately, the thought was, "I know some people who are Influencers. But that's not me."

A few days after the event, I purchased the book and took the assessment. The result for role #1 was *Pioneer*. That made sense because being a pioneer and innovator has always been my sweet spot. A Pioneer is also someone who is optimistic and sees the world as a friendly place. Sounds like me! Then, there was the second role. Can you guess what it was? Yep, you are right. Influencer!

The interesting part is that the assessment results say an influencer is someone who convinces people to act and is persuasive. That is a definition I can identify with and it is only a minor tweak to what was said at the event. However, I decided to dig deeper and see what else there was to know.

The first thing to review was my 30-second commercial. Turns out, there were three (yes 3) separate statements in that 30-second commercial that could be considered a *close*.

For someone who did not think they were always asking for a close it was a big surprise. It is a great example of where an assessment like this opens your eyes to how others *do* see you versus how you think others see you.

This triggered a decision point. Either; accept and embrace being an influencer or keep lying to myself and trying to fool everyone else. Which choice do you think was the winner? You guessed it. Embracing the inner influencer! As in any process of change and discovery, that was only the start of things.

After embracing the inner influencer, a new 30-second commercial was written and other new materials were created. While this was not an overnight process, it provided tons of valuable experiences that will be passed on to you. Some of these are intertwined in this book, others are included in webinars and teleseminars and still others are used in live speaking engagements.

At the time this book was written, I was not an affiliate for the producers of the StandOut® assessment. However, The BE A Success Academy, which we will review later, goes into much more detail on this and other assessments.

Now that you understand the basics behind the Hidden Barrier to More (_____*) #1: Being Incongruous and the key to overcoming this barrier, understanding and accepting who you are, we will move on to the Hidden Barrier to More (_____*) #2: Anticipating the Result.

Hidden Barrier to More (_____*) #2: Anticipating the Result

Picture this; you have 5 conversations with a potential customer and everything is going great. It is going so great that the customer says they look forward to working with you and doing great things together. They ask for one more meeting and you *feel* it is to *seal the deal*. Ask yourself these questions:

> *How would you be feeling walking into that last meeting?*
>
> *What would you be thinking walking into that last meeting?*
>
> *How sure would you be that you were going to win the contract?*
>
> *What mood would you be in right before the meeting?*

If you are like most people, you would be feeling very confident that you were about to win the deal and sign a new customer. In fact, you may even be counting your commissions and figuring out what you are going to buy with your bonus.

On the other hand, you may be thinking like many seasoned sales professionals who say they wait until the ink is dry on the contract before getting too excited. That way of thinking is great and it would be even better if it were only that easy. For those of you who are thinking right now, "It *is* just that easy. Any sales person in their right mind would never count on a sale before the ink is dry." Here is a challenge for you. Continue reading this chapter. It is sure to be an eye opening experience.

One thing you need to understand is that it is human nature to want to predict and expect the outcome. It is built into your DNA to figure things like this out. It is all because your ancestors needed to anticipate the result of every situation in order to stay alive. The good news for most of us is that we are not in life and death situations on a regular basis. On the other hand, things like paying the mortgage, putting the children through school or completing that much needed home repair sometimes tricks your brain into acting the same way.

Anything in your life that causes stress can and usually does initiate the fight-or-flight response. While sometimes it is not as severe as actual *fight* or *flight*, it has the same outcome. Your brain shifts into a mode where it thinks you may need to make a quick decision in order to survive and it begins to try and anticipate the results. Remember, both positive and negative things can act as stressors.   As an example; if you are working on a contract that will net you a $50,000 bonus and you can use that bonus to pay off some debt, while it is a very positive thing, it will be translated into a stressor by your brain.

So, how can you fight this and overcome this hidden barrier?

Transform Your Thinking

Overcoming Barrier #2:
Transform Your Thinking

To permanently overcome the hidden barrier of anticipating the results or the outcome you must *in no uncertain terms* transform your thinking and shift your mindset. Section 2 of this book goes into greater detail on processes to transform your thinking. However, for this hidden barrier, there are three methods specifically designed to transform your thinking around the concept of anticipating the results. These three methods are:

- ✓ Method #1: You talk about getting the opposite result.
- ✓ Method #2: You attach yourself to the process and not the outcome.
- ✓ Method #3: You use the Penalty Jar.

These three methods will start you down the path of transforming your thinking and get you over the biggest obstacles when it comes to anticipating your results.

Once you have had a chance to read this section and use the methods, share your story by visiting this site.

http://TheSecretBlueprintToMore.com/transform

Method #1: You talk about getting the opposite result.

For those of you who are students of the Law of Attraction, this may seem counter-intuitive. However, what you are doing is bringing balance to the situation. If you think you are going to win the contract, talk as if you are not going to win or at least only have a 50/50 chance. Take heart, you only have to do this long enough to convince your subconscious not to betray you and long enough to get you out of the habit of anticipating the result.

For this method, clients usually interpret *talking* loosely. Talking could mean talking to someone else, talking out loud to no one in particular or writing about the result. Clients who do talk to someone about getting the opposite result report that they have the most success by letting the other person know exactly what they are doing. They let the person know that they are working on transforming the way they think in an effort to increase their level of success.

There have been reports of clients getting negative feedback and hearing, *"You should not talk negatively about yourself."* The best way to overcome that is to agree with the person and then explain to them that you have had challenges in the past with anticipating results and you are just trying something different.

Method #2: You attach yourself to the process and not the outcome.

For many clients, this one is easier said than done. They start off by focusing on the thrill of the close or the charge they get when a sale, project or other large task is complete. In this economy, it is also understandable that many clients focus on the money they make when things go right (like bonuses, commissions, etc.).   They focus on the great compliments they receive or the promotions they may get. Some focus on making their first million dollars or being on television or radio for the first time.

What do all of the above things have in common?

They are results and not processes. However, can you blame anyone? We live in a results focused world where you are not applauded for how you run the race (the process) only for where you finish (the result).   Do not misunderstand me. Results are very important and must be achieved.   However, when it comes to reaching a higher level of success, embrace the process and the results will follow.

Every time you think about the result, be it positive or negative, catch yourself, re-set and think about the process. Make the process fun, exciting or whatever you want. The key is to focus on the process and not the outcome.

Method #3: You use the Penalty Jar.

This is a longer process that uses both visual cues and a reward and penalty structure.

> Step #1: Get a jar or some other container and label it The Penalty Jar.

> Step #2: Every time you think you know what the result of a contract, project, task, etc. will be, put a marble, stone, coin, dollar bill or some other object into the jar.

> Step #3: On a weekly basis, empty the jar and count the number of items in it. Your goal should be to reduce the amount of items in the jar on a weekly basis.

> Step #4: Attach a reward and a penalty to the results. If your count went down from the previous week, give yourself the reward, if your count went up, asses yourself the penalty. You choose the reward and the penalty. The reward must be sufficient enough to nudge you in the direction of completing your goal and the penalty must

be sufficient enough to nudge you the direction of completing your goal.

Step #5: Continue until you have two weeks straight of positive results and then your new goal is to reduce your count by 50% each week.

Step #6: Continue until you have two weeks straight of positive results and then your new goal is to reduce your count by 75% each week.

Step #7: Continue until you have two weeks straight of positive results and then your new goal is to reduce your count by 90% each week.

Step #8: Continue until you have two weeks straight of positive results and then your new goal is to have zero objects in the penalty jar.

Remember, this is a process and you are creating a new habit.

So far, we have reviewed two of the Hidden Barriers to More (_____*) that everyone faces and we have seen different ways to overcome each barrier. Now it is time for Hidden Barrier to More (_____*) #3: Giving an Overly Explanatory Explanation.

Hidden Barrier to More (_____*) #3: Giving an Overly Explanatory Explanation

When someone explains things they do not need to, explains things before being asked for an explanation or uses one hundred words to explain something that could be explained in fifty or less, the listener gets the impression, consciously or subconsciously, that they are being lied to or that someone is trying to cover something up.

Most people who fall into this trap think they are just being completely open, honest and upfront with everything. In other words, exactly the opposite of what their listeners perceive. Some people also feel more comfortable giving information and explaining things upfront rather than answering questions on the backend. You need to understand how your listener receives this and what their subconscious does with the information they receive.

We as human beings like to be in control of most situations. When the person speaking has given the listener all the information the speaker has and has not allowed the listener any room to ask any questions, the speaker is in complete control. If you are the one doing the talking, while this may be comfortable for you, the focus should be on your listener and not on you. Your listener is the one you are trying to get to spend money on your product or service, not you.

The other thing that invariably happens is that, if the listener does come up with a question or two, they are usually the toughest ones and the ones most people would probably rather not answer.

Why does this happen?

The brain of the listener is trying to do what it can to be in control and it is looking for the answer to the question, *"What is missing?"* The brain of the speaker is trying to be in control and anticipate everything.

Once again, it is not your fault. Much of why you do this can be attributed to your years in school and the *500 word essays* you wrote. You were taught from an early age that, when you are given a subject, you need to come up with a certain amount of words and put in all the information you could. This was true even if you ended up repeating yourself. Most people were not taught to give the right amount of information. They were taught to give as much information as possible.

So, how do you overcome this barrier?

Write out the Details

Overcoming Barrier #3:
Write Out the Details

Warning: This method is going to sound counterintuitive to many people. In fact, during the writing of this book, a few people I showed it to laughed at the title of this section and questioned the process. They said things like, "To get over being overly explanatory, you want us to completely outline everything and *be* overly explanatory?" You got it!

The reason is that you cannot change any habit, thought or way of doing something without accepting that you are doing it and allowing it to be *ok* with your brain. There is an old saying that *force negates* and it is very applicable in a case like this. If you try and force a change on yourself, your brain will automatically reject it. However, if you give yourself permission to be a certain way and then find ways to nudge your brain in the direction you want it to go, success is sure to follow. Now we will get on to the process.

> Step #1: Write out everything you are going
> to give a prospective customer in a bulleted
> list. This includes every statement, every

piece of marketing literature, every reference, everything. Do not leave anything out.

Step #2: Put four columns to the right of each piece of information.

Step #3: Label each of the columns as follows.

Column 1: Amount of Content
Column 2: Level of Content
Column 3: Impact of Content
Column 4: Priority Ranking

Step #4: Rank each piece of information on a scale from 1 to 10 as follows.

Amount: 1 = Extra Large; 10 = Very Small
Level: 1 = Very Detail; 10 = Very High Level Summary
Impact: 1 = Very Low; 10 = Very High

Step #5: Multiply all three columns to get a final result and put it in the Priority Ranking column.

Step #6: Reorder the information by Priority Ranking from highest to lowest value.

Step #7: Take only the top 50% of the information and give it to your next 10 potential customers.

Step #8: If your customers still are not asking a lot of questions and your close rate has not gone up, pick ½ of the list you are currently using and replace it with the top ½ of the list you are not currently using.

Step #9: Present the new information to your next 10 potential customers.

Step #10: Based on your results, continue tweaking the amount of information you are giving prospective customers so that, over time, the following happens.

✓ Phase #1: 75% of the time you are doing the talking, 25% of the time the customer is asking questions.

- ✓ Phase #2: 50% of the time you are doing the talking, 50% of the time the customer is asking questions.
- ✓ Phase #3: 25% of the time you are doing the talking, 75% of the time the customer is asking questions.
- ✓ Phase #4: 10% of the time you are doing the talking, 90 % of the time the customer is asking questions.

If at this point you are still struggling, you are probably not giving your customers the information they want or need. To overcome this, you will need to take a more direct approach and survey your existing customers or clients.

Note: If you are not a sales professional, this method still applies to you. Regardless of what profession you are in, everyone has some sort of customer or client.

Your existing customers are the best source of information when it comes to understanding the unique aspects your product, service, organization or company brings to the market place. They are also the best source of information as to what made them choose you over the other competitors. When surveying your customers, use the 80/20 rule. Interview the Top 20% of your customers, the ones that provide 80% of your revenue.

If you are going to get more customers, you want to get those customers who will bring you the greatest return, right?

If you work in a corporate environment (think project manager), you will be looking at the people who control the majority of the budget (time or money) or the groups that make the biggest impact on the bottom line of the company.

Here are some additional things this scenario and asking questions in general, will provide you.

- ✓ The prospective customer will tell you what is important to them.
- ✓ You can tailor your offering to meet their needs.
- ✓ You have a better chance earlier on to prequalify your potential clients and/or customers.

Since we are now 1/3rd of the way through the hidden barriers, here is a question for you.

How are you doing so far?

Share your experiences by visiting:

http://TheSecretBlueprintToMore.com/write

32 The Secret Blueprint to More (_____*)

We have now reviewed three of the Hidden Barriers to More (_____*) and we have seen different ways to overcome each barrier. Now, we will move on to Hidden Barrier to More (_____*) #4: Using the Dreaded 'ly' Words.

Hidden Barrier to More (_____*) #4: Using the Dreaded 'ly' Words

Really, while words that end in 'ly' are usually wonderfully appropriate to use and in most circumstances it is totally and absolutely appropriate to use words that end in 'ly', you may be inadvertently or accidentally giving a partially incorrect impression to your listener.

For many years, police officers have used a very simple tactic to know when people are lying. The person prefaces their statement with a word ending in 'ly'. While not everyone who uses words ending in 'ly' is lying, more often than not they are trying to make something sound better than it is or they are trying to hide something.

Ask yourself this: What were you thinking while you were reading all of the 'ly' words at the beginning of this module? Other than possibly being irritated, if you are like most people, you *sensed* something was not right or it did not feel comfortable to you. We will take this one step further and examine some other things that people say.

When someone says, "Really, I'm telling you the truth." the subconscious of the listener translates it two ways. First, the subconscious sends up a red flag and thinks, "So, you do not always tell the truth?"   The second signal the subconscious gets is that the person speaking is trying to convince or persuade the listener that they are being honest.

When someone says, "I have absolutely no idea what you are talking about." the subconscious of the listener immediately perks up and wonders why the person speaking need to qualify *no idea*. It thinks, "Isn't *no idea* plain enough?" You either have some idea or no idea, there is not much in-between.

When someone says, "I have basically no idea what you mean." the subconscious of the listener correctly picks up on the fact that the person speaking has some idea what the listener means.   However, they have a limited understanding.

When someone says, "I literally spent hours waiting for this to get done." the subconscious of the listener picks up on the fact that the person had to wait. However, more often than not the subconscious thinks that the person did not wait for *hours.* Maybe they waited for an hour or two, but not the many hours the statement implies.

Remember, this is the subconscious picking up on these things and not the conscious mind. This means that the listener more often than not will not fully understand why they are questioning the speaker and may just get the *feeling* that they do not want to do business with the speaker. Ask yourself the following question.

Have you ever been in a situation where you just felt something was wrong and could not identify what was wrong?

If so, then you experienced your subconscious kicking in and trying to protect you. You either picked up on the micro-expressions of the speaker or that they were using overly descriptive words.

The challenge is that most people are not in-tune with their inner subconscious enough to ask *why* and will not give someone the chance to prove they are not trying to lie to them, hide something from them or being deceitful. They will just move on. This barrier goes hand-in-hand with Hidden Barrier to More (_____*) #3: Giving an Overly Explanatory Explanation.

So, how do you break through this barrier?

Listen to Yourself and Learn

Overcoming Barrier #4:
Listen to Yourself and Learn

Step #1: Get a hand-held voice recorder. To get started, you could use your smartphone or tablet.   However, a voice recorder is better because it allows you to eventually give yourself time to unplug and focus on changing this habit.   Section 2 devotes a whole chapter to recording your thoughts and why it is critical to unplug. For now, the short version is that only when you unplug from your phone, tablet, etc. can you use 100% of your mental capacity.   While this exercise may not require that level of concentration, we are also building good habits and a hand-held voice recorder is a good habit.

Step #2: Record your elevator speech and determine how many 'ly' words you use.

Step #3: Record your sales pitch and determine how many 'ly' words you use.

Step #4: Rewrite both your elevator speech and sales pitch and reduce the number of 'ly' words by 50%.

Step #5: Test your newly updated elevator speech and sales pitch on your next 10 potential customers.

Step #6: Continue to refine both your elevator speech and sales pitch by eliminating words that end in 'ly' until you reach your desired close ratio.

If your close ratio is still not where you want it to be, invest in a business coach to help you refine your message and say the right thing with the right amount of words.

Congratulations, four barriers down and five to go. Next, we will move on to Hidden Barrier to More (_____*) #5: Trying to Get Married Before Dating.

Hidden Barrier to More (_____*) #5: Trying to Get Married Before Dating

Ask yourself the following questions:

> *Would you ask a woman or man to marry you within the first 30 seconds after you meet them?*
>
> *Would you ask someone to do business with you after knowing them for only 30 seconds?*
>
> *Do you know as soon as you meet someone if you want to do business with them or not?*

If you are like the majority of people, you answered *no* to the first two questions. The third one is a bit trickier. This is because, sometimes, when we meet someone, we know instantly that we will not be doing business with them. We just do not get a good vibe or a good feeling. It usually comes in the form of us thinking, "There is something not right." and it is not apparent what is not right. However, less common is the person who knows they will do business with someone they just met. For those of you who *know* you are going to do business with someone right after meeting them ask yourself this question.

Do you think you are sending off signals to a person you just met that you want to do business with them?

While you need to know if you *may* do business with someone you meet, there is a big difference between knowing you *will* and knowing you *may*.

Many people pride themselves on being a great judge of character and knowing within the first 30 seconds whether or not they are going to do business with someone. The problem is that most people are not that way and are resistant to people who try and push hard after the first meeting. Sometimes it is taken as desperate and other times the person cannot explain it.

Many of my clients have struggled with this barrier because it is so easy to fall into and it is difficult to get out once you have fallen in. This is because when two people meet and one realizes that doing business with the other one would be great for their business, their mind starts turning and trying to figure out how to make the business connection last.

What is even more of a challenge is someone who always tries to develop a business relationship and never a friendship. The following is a story of a first-hand experience. Share stories about your first-hand experiences by visiting:

http://TheSecretBlueprintToMore.com/focus

Once, a fellow professional speaker who is very successful saw me speak and was very complimentary afterwards. This person makes a living as a speaker and an impersonator because he looks exactly like another very famous person. Because of the predisposition to the *Married Before You Date* syndrome, when we talked, I said, "One day, I would love to share the stage with you as *you.*" The point was supposed to be that doing an event with this person as themselves and not their *character* would be great. Their reaction was a surprise. They said, "Whoa, hold on a minute. Let's share fellowship first and see where that goes."

This situation made me look at other relationships and realize that every relationship I started was starting from a business standpoint and not a personal standpoint. Funny thing is that the one recent relationship where business was an afterthought has turned into one of the best business and personal relationships I have had in a long while. The down-side is this, who knows how many other relationships could have been built if *dating* a prospective client would have happened before trying to *marry* them.

The tricky thing is that, if you are like many other people and you are always thinking a few steps ahead, you are going to find it hard to get used to dating before marriage.

There is another reason that people give off the feeling or perception that they are trying to get married before they date. This one goes back to childhood and the interaction between children as they grow up. Some people have a difficult time growing up relating to other children. In the old days, there was even a space on school report cards labeled *Plays Well with Others*. Children who have difficulty *playing well with others* are predisposed to grow up to be adults who focus on business relationships first and then personal relationships.

Why does this happen?

It is all a matter of repetition and experiences. If someone struggles to *play well with others*, their brain gets constant reinforcement that they are no good at personal relationships because all relationships as children are *personal*. When they move into adulthood, they begin to experience success in a business environment. It may be getting the first job they apply to or getting their first promotion. Whatever the case, if someone who experienced challenges as a child in personal relationships has success when they hit the business world, there is a very good chance that they will focus on business relationships first and personal relationships second.

How do you get over this barrier?

Focus on the Present

Overcoming Barrier #5:
Focus on the Present

To break through this barrier and focus on dating a prospective client before you *marry* them, you need to concentrate on the present while thinking about the future. This is easier said than done. To do this effectively, you must give your complete focus to the conversation you are having with the person. While this sounds simple, try some time to give 100% focus to everything the person you meet is saying. Do not translate what they are saying into how it may help you in the future. Do not think of all of the possibilities that a business relationship with your new found acquaintance may mean for you. Remember, the reason you are talking to the person is because you have identified them as a possible match for your business. Whether you did it consciously or subconsciously does not matter.

When first trying to overcome this barrier, some clients report great success when they open up and tell people they meet about what they are doing and let the people know that they are trying to get to know people at a more personal level before doing business with them. However, this can be challenging for some people because it involves being transparent to someone you just met. Simply put, it is being open enough to tell someone you just met that when you meet people, most of the time you focus on business first and then the personal side of things later.

The good news is that, one of two things will happen. Either the person will thank you for telling them and things will progress nicely, or the person will move on. Either result is good for you. If they thank you for telling them, you have the chance to build a good business relationship and possible friendship. If they do not say anything or move on quickly, they are not a good fit for you and where you are at now. The even better news is that you do not have to spend time with someone who is not a good fit for you. The great news is that, as you change, if you were meant to have a business or personal relationship with that person, you will meet them again and be able to show them that you have changed.

For those who want or need outside help to get over this obstacle, welcome to the majority! This is a great time to consider hiring a coach to help you understand and embrace why you do what you do, work with you to change what you are doing and empower you to succeed.

Next, we will move on to Hidden Barrier to More (_____*) #6: Focusing on You and not Your Client.

Hidden Barrier to More (_____*) #6: Focusing on You and not Your Client

Ask yourself the following question.

Is everything about you?

Many people know the key to successfully connecting with others (and in-turn the key to success in business) is to always remember that it is all about the other person. Whether it is a conversation, email, blog post or article, you need to forget about what you want and focus on what the listener, reader, customer, client, etc. wants. This is not a case of telling them what they *want* to hear, like when you just agree with someone to stop an argument. This is a case of telling them what they need to hear in a way that they will receive it. This is not necessarily the way you would receive it and not necessarily the way you want to say it.

Here is an example. Say you are in France and you speak some French, not a lot, but enough to get by. You come upon a local French citizen and need to get directions to the nearest restaurant. Your natural instinct may be to ask the question in English hoping that the person understands English. Another thought may be to ask them if they speak English.

Both of these scenarios fall into the bucket of focusing on you and not your client. However, if you think in terms of focusing on your client, you will at least try to ask the question in French. The great news is that, if both of you are thinking in terms of your client, the person you just met will realize that you are struggling with French. If they know English, they will respond to you in English.

Here is the challenge, not all situations are as easy as the one above to identify whether we are doing things the way we want to do them or doing things the way our listener wants to see them done.

If we know we should always focus on the other person,
why do some people find it difficult to do?

The answer is human nature. Many years ago, we needed to be self-sufficient to survive. We needed to be in control of our life and our surroundings. However, as time passed, things changed and people started to realize that working together and thinking about other people is a better way to survive. The bad news is that this has only been a recent revelation and we have thousands of years of history to overcome.

The good news is that you can overcome it. The key to overcoming this barrier is objectively determining if you are focusing on you or your client. Objectivity is the key here. This is because when asked if they focus on themselves or the other person, at least 90% of people say they focus on the other person. However, after running a few tests, it becomes obvious that the percentage is closer to 20% than it is to 90%.

To objectively identify when you are focusing on you and when you are focusing on your client, first you need to identify your predisposition. In other words, are you predisposed to focusing on you or your client?

How do you find out if you are predisposed to focus on you or your client?

Complete the following 5 Project Review

Overcoming Barrier #6:
The 5 Project Review

Remember, the first step to changing anything is to understand yourself and what needs to be changed.

Step #1: Take 5 sheets of paper or use your favorite computer program. On the top of each page, write a general overview of each of the last 5 projects or tasks you worked on.

Step #2: Divide the paper into two columns.

Step #3: Label the two columns as follows.

Column #1: General Consensus
Column #2: What was Done

Step #4: In the *General Consensus* column, list what your customers, other experts, the general public, etc. think should be done to make the project or task a success.

Step #5: In the *What was Done* column; write what you did in an effort to make the project or task a success.

Step #6: Compare the two lists and cross off anything that appears exactly the same in both. In other words, cross off any time you did what everyone else would have done.

Step #7: Review all remaining items and ensure a one-to-one match. If something in one column has no match in the other, dig deeper and do research to come up with the match.

Step #8: Take a look at the differences and be objective.   Ask yourself the following questions:

Did what you did make the project better or worse than it would have been if you would have done what everyone else suggested?

Did you receive positive or negative feedback?

Did you secure more referrals?

Did you receive any calls?

Step #9: Find publicly available metrics on your project and compare them to your results.

Were your results better or worse than the average?

If your results were better than the average, great! Keep doing what you are doing. If your results fell short of the industry average, you have got some work to do.

If you found in Step #9 you needed to change a few things, here are a few steps to start making those changes.

Step #10: Determine which two things you need to change will give you the biggest return on your investment.

Step #11: Change those two things on your next project.

Step #12: Review your results.

If you are still not getting the results you desire, repeat steps #10 through #12 until you get the desired results.

We are now 2/3^{rds} of the way through the Hidden Barriers to More (_____*) and here is a question for you.

How are you doing so far?

Share your experiences by visiting:

http://TheSecretBlueprintToMore.com/projectreview

So far, we have reviewed six of the Hidden Barriers to More (_____*) that everyone faces and we have seen different ways to overcome each barrier. Now, it is time for Hidden Barrier to More (_____*) #7: Using up All Your Energy on *Busy Work*.

Hidden Barrier to More (_____*) #7: Using up All Your Energy on *Busy Work*

While people easily understand that we only have a limited amount of time in a given day, the concept many people struggle with is that we only have a limited amount of mental energy in a given day.

When most people think of energy, they think of physical energy. Physical energy is easy to quantify. You can only run, walk or do any physical activity for a given period of time, until you are tired and worn-out. Think about the last time you shoveled snow off of your driveway or mowed your lawn and it is easy to understand that we only have a limited amount of physical energy in a given day. Ask yourself the following question.

When is the last time you remember feeling mentally tired?

Most people do not correlate the tired feeling they have at the end of the day with being mentally tired. However, in many cases, that is what it is. Studies have shown that you burn calories while thinking. Since calories = energy, it stands to reason that you are using energy while thinking.

Because most people do not know about this or do not make the connection between mental activity and using up energy, they spend a major portion of their day doing *busy work* or doing things that are not critical to their success. If you are an entrepreneur, this can be a big challenge, especially if you are in an early stage start-up and are working with limited funds. Entrepreneurs in that scenario feel they need to do everything in the business themselves. It could be in an effort to save money or just because they have fun doing the things.

For everyone, things like emails, phone calls, tweets, text messages and all of the other wonderful things the technology age has given us make it very easy to get distracted and use a large amount of energy on busy work. Studies show that an interruption in your concentration when working on a task can cost you an extra 10 to 20 minutes *above* the amount of time spent on the distraction. This comes from the time it takes to get back to what you were doing and get the momentum back you lost.

Why do people let themselves get distracted?

Everyone likes to feel important. Mind you, this is different from being famous. Being important is having the feeling that someone needs you. It is human nature to like the feeling of being needed. The fact that we like to feel needed, drives us to do many things. While most of them are harmless on the surface, they could be doing major damage to your productivity and your success. Some examples of *busy work* are:

- ✓ Answering all emails right away.
- ✓ Having all emails give you a reminder that they are in your inbox.
- ✓ Answering all phone calls.
- ✓ Having your door open the entire work day.
- ✓ Opening the mail.

Notice the specific language used: *All emails, all phone calls, entire work day.* Everyone knows that there are critical issues that happen during a day. For critical issues, one suggestion is to put a plan in place to handle as many of them as possible before they become a distraction and set aside time in the day to handle *busy work* tasks in groups.

How do you overcome using up all your energy on busy work?

Do the Big Things First

Overcoming Barrier #7:
Do the Big Things First

There are three elements to the concept of doing the big things first that will take you from doing things yourself to delegating. The three elements are:

- ✓ Have a plan.
- ✓ Designate time for the small things.
- ✓ Hire and delegate.

We will now look at each element in a bit more depth.

Element #1: Have a plan.

To capitalize on your precious mental energy, you need to have a solid plan for each day and ensure you take care of breaking up your biggest and nastiest rocks at the beginning of the day and then take care of the smaller ones if energy permits. Doing less and focusing on the big things first is counterintuitive to many people who feel that getting many things done equates to more progress than getting one big thing done. In most cases, the opposite is true.

Both the need to get many things done and the need to focus on the quantity of work done get ingrained at a very young age into the way most people do things. During their early, formative years, school children are asked to complete homework assignments for many classes each day and each week. If they do not do all of them, they are penalized. This puts the focus on getting everything done, regardless if it is big or small.

There is usually no prioritization of assignments or the ability to get some things done and not others. While some people say this teaches children how to handle many things, get them all done and teaches them responsibility (which does have some merit), they do not realize that the children are also being taught to worry about getting many things done versus concentrating on getting the most important things done.

One way parents try to overcome this is to have children do their homework before they go out to play. In theory, this is great because parents are trying to teach their kids to do what is most important or what will give them the best return on their time investment first and do everything else second. The parents who succeed at doing this are the ones with children who understand that schoolwork is more important than playing. Without digressing too much more, suffice it to say that what happens when we are young can have a major impact on the rest of our lives.

*What does this predisposition to getting many things
done have to do with planning?*

When we plan our day, we have more control over
where and how we spend our time. Unless we already have
a meeting booked, we can control when we work on things,
the amount of energy we give to each task and we can block
out time to work on certain things. Here are some tips on
successful time planning.

- ✓ Block out time in at least 45 minute increments
  with the optimal time being around an hour.
- ✓ Take a break at the end of each block of time so
  that you stay fresh.
- ✓ If a task will take longer than an hour, break it
  down into 45 minute chunks.
- ✓ Decide which task you have on your list will
  give you the biggest return on your investment
  and commit to starting it first the next morning.
- ✓ Commit to working on that one big task until it
  is done. If you need the help of someone else,
  commit to getting the task to a point where you
  can send it off to the other person.
- ✓ Be realistic and commit to getting things done.
- ✓ Schedule time for *other* things. This is one of the
  key elements to doing the big things first, so we
  will go deeper.

<u>Element #2: Designate time for *other* things.</u>

While working on the biggest rocks at the beginning of the day is great, people who do not schedule a little time to do *other* things run into the problem that their brain or subconscious worries about the other things that are not getting done or they worry about the amount of things getting done. This could be just as detrimental to your success as only focusing on the little things.

The keys to successfully designating time for other things are:

- ✓ Plan the time at the end of the day.
- ✓ If you run out of mental energy, do not beat yourself up. Move the tasks to the end of the following day.
- ✓ If you need to move the tasks, do not put them at the beginning of the day. It will defeat the purpose of why you are doing the big things first.
- ✓ If you are going to commit to someone that you will get something done that is low on the priority list, give yourself enough room so that it will not all of a sudden become a high priority.
- ✓ When it comes to email, plan a time to check your email each day. The later in the day the better. Setup a system with your clients so that

they will know how to get a hold of you if something critical comes up. One way that has been successful is using an *out-of-office* type of auto response to emails telling the sender that in order to serve all your customers better, you check emails only once per day and if they need an answer faster, they can call you. The trick here is to give them a phone number for critical issues that is different than your usual phone number. This way, you will get used to answering the critical issue phone and leaving everything else go to voicemail when you are in the middle of one of your time blocks.

✓ When it comes to voicemails, plan a block of time to return phone calls. This is one task you should not move. It gives many people who reach out by phone a negative impression if you do not reach back out the same day. However, this does not mean you need to have a long conversation with the person. If you are in the middle of one of your big rocks and need a few days to get it done, tell the person that in such a way that does not leave them thinking they are second best.

✓ When it comes to an open door policy, plan a block of time when your door is closed and you should not be disturbed except for very critical issues. Some of the best managers I have known have used this method and it works like a charm.

Element #3: Hire and Delegate.

Much of the *busy work* you do could be delegated to someone else so that only the big things hit your plate. For entrepreneurs in the start-up phase, this could be a big challenge. One way to overcome this challenge is to hire a virtual assistant. Virtual assistants can be either on-shore or off-shore and can do a lot to free-up your time. Here is a question for you.

If you are making $100 an hour, why would you do something that you could pay someone else $10 an hour to do?

The logical answer may be that the $10/hour is not in the budget but the hour of time can be pulled from something else. Speaking from personal experience I would question that and challenge you to find out a way to be able to afford paying someone to do some of the tasks that yield a low return on your personal time investment.

Seven down, two to go. Next, we will move on to the Hidden Barrier to More (_____*) #8: Your Timing is Off.

Hidden Barrier to More (_____*) #8: Your Timing is Off

Timing here means that you only do things or think about doing things when you know they will not succeed. It is very easy at 3am to think about all the great things that can be done the following morning. Then, the day rolls around and the things do not get done. Now, we will take a look at a real world scenario.

One client, we will call him James (not his real name) had a fear of talking on the phone, unless someone called him. This was a big problem since the quickest way for him to get business was to either cold call or warm call people. It is understandable that cold calling is something that he did not like to do. There is the fear of rejection and the assumption most people place on cold calling or telemarketing. However, he was even afraid to warm call. In this case, his warm calls were people who his friends or acquaintances told him about and were people who were sometimes even expecting his call. Think about that for a second. There were people expecting his call that he would not reach out to.

After working with James for a while, he opened up and said that at night he would always plan to call these people the next day. However, he admitted that he never followed through with his plan. Things eventually got so bad that he stopped returning phone calls period. The only way anyone could get him on the phone was if they called him and he answered the call or if they setup a meeting with him. While this is an effective time management strategy, for James, it went much deeper.

Other clients relate that they cannot see themselves getting this bad. They feel that, as soon as push comes to shove they will magically change and be someone who can get their timing right. While the change will feel like it happens in an instant, it does take some time to readjust your timing and get things right. Here is why.

The reason your timing is off is because when thinking about something and making the decision to do it when there is no possibility of doing it at that very moment, your fear barrier is down and your brain is not scared of failing. However, when the next day rolls around and your subconscious starts thinking about the possibility of failing and how much failing would *hurt*, it springs into action in an attempt to protect you. This protection could come in the form of:

✓ Starting a lower risk, lower cost task first thing in the morning and allowing it to take much longer than it needs to.

✓ Allowing any interruption to distract you from the task.

✓ Coming up with any excuse or reason not to do the task.

✓ Rationalizing not doing the task because something else is more important.

✓ Giving more importance than necessary to a less important task.

<u>Here is an example.</u>

Say you are faced with the choice of going to the dentist to get a root canal or going to see a sporting event. Obviously, the root canal will be painful. However, it will also bring you relief once it is done. On the other hand, the sporting event has more of a chance of bringing you joy because your team is the best in the league this year and the team they are playing is the worst.

The night before the game, most people think, "Ok. I am going to finally go to the dentist tomorrow and get this tooth fixed. I do not have tickets to the game anyway and while the dentist will be painful, it will be worth it." The next day rolls around and the fear of going to the dentist kicks in. Then, people start looking at online ticket sellers to find a pair of tickets for the game. They finally find a pair of tickets. They buy them and change their appointment. The person who does this allows fear to take over and does the less important thing of seeing the sporting event override the more important task of getting his or her tooth fixed.

Think about situations in your own life and ask yourself these questions:

Are there times when you decide to do a task that is less important only to avoid doing one that could be painful?

Are there times when you rationalize doing one task over another? (Hint: If you have to rationalize doing one task over another, it often means the task you are not doing may cause pain. It could also be showing you that your subconscious is experiencing fear.)

When have you decided to do something overnight and then did not follow-through the next day. Why did you not follow-through?

How do you get over this barrier?

Reflect and Plan with a Purpose

Overcoming Barrier #8:
Reflect and Plan with a Purpose

To get over this barrier you need to reflect and plan with a purpose and commit to the plan. You may even want to get an accountability partner. Before we go into why this is important and exactly how to do it, we will focus on accountability for a moment.

Accountability can be positive for some people and negative for others. Many clients admit to needing accountability. They also say that it is much harder for them to avoid doing something if someone else is expecting them to do it than it is if only they are expecting themselves to do it.

However, some clients take the opposite approach. They have difficulty utilizing an accountability partner. They feel that the goal stops being their own when they have an accountability partner. What we work on in The BE A Success Academy is that the problem is not in having accountability or in the accountability relationship; it is in the goals a person sets for themselves. The trick is to ensure you really want to achieve the goal you set for yourself and then have someone hold you accountable for it. The next chapter will cover this in more detail. For now, we will get back to what it means to reflect and plan with a purpose.

To reflect and plan with a purpose, you need to think about the things that scare you at a time when you know you cannot do them (when your fear barrier is at its least) and then put a plan in place for doing those things when you can do them. For example, most people will not be making phone calls to prospective clients at 11:00 at night. Some people may say they will because they know the call is going to the office. The challenge is that people can have their office phones transferred to their home phones. What is worse than not calling a prospective client? Calling them late at night, that is what. Here is a step-by-step process.

> Step #1: At a time when you know you cannot do anything, make a list of all of those things you know you should do but are too scared to do.

> Step #2: Put four columns to the right of each piece of information.

> Step #3: Label each of the columns as follows.

> Column 1: Return on Investment
> Column 2: Level of Fear

Column 3: Impact of the Change

Column 4: Priority Ranking

Step #4: Rank each piece of information on a scale from 1 to 10 as follows.

Return on Investment:

1 = Very Low; 10 = Very High

Level of Fear:

1 = Very Low; 10 = Very High

Impact of the Change:

1 = Very Low; 10 = Very High

Step #5: Multiply all three columns to get a final result and put it in the Priority Ranking column.

Step #6: Reorder the information by Priority Ranking from highest to lowest value.

Step #7: Create a plan with the task that is now #1 on your list being the primary thing you will get done.

Step #8: Execute the plan the next business day.

> Step #9: At the end of the next business day, reflect on the achievements from the day and. As long as task #1 is done, put a new plan in place for task #2.

> Step #10: Execute the new plan the next business day.

Continue to reflect and plan with a purpose on a daily basis until you overcome your fears. We go into much more detail on reflecting and planning in section two of this book. For now, remember that reflecting and planning needs to be a daily happening and it will serve to keep you on the track to success. Oh yeah, and one more thing. If you do not fill your schedule with what is important to you, other people will find a way to fill your schedule with what is important to them. This is another reason planning is so important.

So far, we have reviewed eight of the Hidden Barriers to More (_____*) that everyone faces and we have seen different ways to overcome each barrier. Now it is time for Hidden Barrier to More (_____*) #9: Chasing the Money and not Your Passion.

Hidden Barrier to More (_____*) #9: Chasing the Money and not Your Passion

First, we will get one thing out of the way. Money is a wonderful thing. However, money is pretty much only good for two things, to make memories and give people options. Included in making memories are things like donating to charity and helping worthy causes. Included in giving people options are things like where to live, what car to drive and what school to send your children to. Notice that we are not talking about driving the most expensive car or have the biggest house. We are only talking about having the choice of where to live and what to drive. The problem is that we need money to survive in this world.

The need to have money becomes a problem when people start running out of money and need to make an idea or a business succeed. It also becomes a problem when people become desperate and have their attention drawn away from what they need to do to succeed. Now, we will look at a case study to find out how money does this.

Case Study: The Struggling Business Owner

One client, we will call him Matt (not his real name), was a struggling business owner. Matt was (and still is) a very creative guy and can see the possibility in any situation. With his business struggles, Matt was always looking for a way to make money. He was always either trying the latest and greatest thing or getting involved in relationship marketing businesses. On top of that, he was in a state of denial about why he was trying all of these different things.

On a regular basis he would look at his love of photography and decide to try and start selling his pictures on line or look at his ability to be creative and create neat sayings and think about starting to sell t-shirts or posters with them on. What made things worse is that he would hear about many different side-businesses and then convince himself he could do that business. He would spend hours researching only to have the passion fade and move on to the next thing.

The problem Matt was facing was that he was chasing the money and not his passion. He never sat down to find out what he was truly passionate about. Since he was not sure what he was truly passionate about, there was no way he could commit to making it a success. Even when he thought he knew what he was passionate about, he could be easily distracted by the next *shiny object*.

Do not misunderstand this barrier. If you are in financial trouble, you will need to do what you have to do to take care of your family. My hope for you is that you can stick to your passion and give it 100%. If that is not possible, you may need to take a detour from your passion and do what you have to do to provide for your family.

Taking a detour is where things become tricky. You need to figure out why you are thinking about doing what you are thinking about doing. To find this out, ask yourself the following questions about what you are thinking about doing.

Is it merely a distraction and something that takes away from your passion?

Is it something that can really generate income?

Is it something that is sustainable?

Is it something that has a legitimate chance of succeeding?

Is it something that you would do even if you were not in desperate need of money?

Is it something that is in direct alignment with your passion?

How do you overcome this barrier?

Use Passion, Strengths and Commitment

Overcoming Barrier #9: Use Passion, Strengths and Commitment

To stop chasing the money, you need to be aware that you are chasing the money, make sure you know exactly what your passion is, make sure you know exactly what your strengths are and then commit to being focused on success.

Step #1: Be self-aware. To start, ask yourself the following questions:

When you browse the internet, does anything that can possibly make you money catch your eye?

While watching TV, do you see offers or commercials that immediately make you think you could do that to make money?

Do you find yourself looking at ways to make money even though you know that you do not fit with what you are looking at? For example: Are you looking at relationship marketing businesses that require you to have home parties and you do not like having people over to your house?

If you answered *yes* to any of the questions in Step #1, chances are you are chasing the money.

Step #2: Unlock you passion. To start, ask yourself the following questions:

What makes you laugh?

What makes you cry?

What would you do even if you did not get paid for it?

If you had to do the same thing for work every day for the rest of your life, what would you do without being bored?

Have people ever told you that you have certain gifts? If so, what were the gifts?

What do you do that seems to make time stand still?

What do you do that you get so involved in that you look at the clock and realize two hours have passed since the last time you looked at the clock?

What do you do when you should be doing something else?

What makes you unique?

What one thing you do would be the toughest for you to give up?

What do you dream about at night?

What do you day dream about?

Step #3: Embrace your strengths.

We have already touched on a number of ways to find your strengths, now it is time to embrace them. Let us say your strength is standing in front of a room full of people and captivating an audience. Let us also say that you are trying unsuccessfully to get coaching clients. If so, figure out why you are trying to get coaching clients. If it is because you think coaching is a quicker way to make money, take a break from trying to get coaching clients, declare yourself a public speaker and put your energy into finding and securing speaking gigs.

Step #4: Commit to success.

Now that you have become self-aware, found your passion and embraced your strengths, commit to success. Commit to spending at least 95% of your time on a daily basis to make your dreams happen. Do this for at least 30 days to ensure you have overcome this barrier and put yourself on the way to success. If you cannot devote 95% of your time on a daily basis to making your dreams happen (for example, you need to take a job to pay the rent), do not beat yourself up. Just realize that it will take you longer to overcome this barrier.

Congratulations! You made it! In Section 1, we focused on understanding and unlocking the Hidden Barriers to More (_____*).

How are you doing so far?

Share your experiences by visiting

http://TheSecretBlueprintToMore.com/keys

Keep reading to find out How to Think Differently.

Section #2: How to Think Differently

"When you change the way you think, the barriers you have melt away." Chris M. Sprague

How to Think Differently: Pre-work: Understand Yourself

In section one, we talked about transforming your mindset being a key to overcoming some of your Hidden Barriers to More (_____*).   Clients love the tools in section one and always ask for more. So, here are some pre-work tasks and 6 additional methods that will help you to Think Differently.

Before trying to Think Differently, you need to understand your current strengths and weaknesses and how they affect both your mindset and the way you currently think. You have already read about multiple ways of understanding your strengths and weaknesses. Whichever way you chose, this understanding is critical to your success. Here are the methods we already discussed.

- ✓ Method #1: Talk about getting the opposite result.
- ✓ Method #2: Be attached to the process and not the outcome.
- ✓ Method #3: Use the Penalty Jar.
- ✓ Method #4: Concentrate on the present while thinking about the future.

How to Think Differently #1:
Do it Twice

Before we dive in to this method, you need to know what this chapter was originally going to be called. It was, *"Do it how you want to do it and then re-do it how people will like it."* However, that was too much of a mouthful (smile). In the end, that is the basic concept we will cover in this method. While it may seem counterintuitive and it may make you cringe that you will have to do more work, bear with the process and try it out. The process will work.

This book is an excellent example of this method in action. It took a long time to start writing this book because one of the original goals was to write it like other authors write their books. The thinking was that I needed to do it once and do it right. Unfortunately, all it did was stop the book from being written at all.

When the epiphany moment finally happened that writing a book needs to be done in a *comfortable* way and that feeling comfortable and getting the book done was more important than doing things right the first time, thoughts began to flow and the book just came out. It allowed years of experience, knowledge, case studies and methods you will use to break through your barriers and succeed to come out.

While you are in the process of transforming your mindset, you may need to do redundant work or do work multiple times. The first time you do the work, you need to do it in a way your brain can relate to. This may mean typing your thoughts down in a free flow format and then going back and reformatting the output to match what your customer wants. It may include talking things out, recording your thoughts and then transcribing them or any number of other things. The most important thing to do is to become ok with the fact that you may have to re-do some work.

Over time, as you move closer to your final mindset shift, one of two things will happen. Either, you will fully understand the way your customers want to see things and do it that way the first time or you will become good enough at doing and redoing things that you will be able to do them twice in the same time it takes your competitors to do it once. However, it usually only takes losing one or two big contracts to transform your mindset and understand that you have to find a way to do your best while giving your clients what they want the first time. The key here is to keep what makes you great and give the customer what they want and expect.

Now, we will move on to how to Create the Right Inner Circle.

How to Think Differently #2: Create the Right Inner Circle

For those of you who have never heard of the concept of an inner circle, it is a group of 5 people who are the closest to you in various areas of your life. You may have an inner circle for business, one for your personal life, one for your hobbies, etc. As an example, if you are a bowler and are on a bowling team, the team would be your bowling inner circle. These are the people you know and the people whose opinions you can trust when it comes to anything bowling-related.

The concept of creating the right inner circle may sound like an easy one. However, there is a way to create an inner circle that will ensure you are able to transform your mindset and break through your barriers. The key to the following process working is to both choose the right people for your inner circle and track the results.

The right people are crucial to this process because, sometimes transforming your mindset can happen in a moment. The moment when you realize someone you respect thinks a certain way or does a certain thing. The reason this can make such a dramatic shift in your mindset is because it gives your brain the permission to do that same thing. Having that permission is a powerful thing.

You will also want to track your results. In order to track your results, record any major decision you need to make. Do this whether or not you take it to your inner circle. Then, record what you initially think the decision will be. Then, record what your decision actually is. Finally, review and understand how your decisions change over time and watch your new way of thinking develop.   Now that you understand the basics, we will move on to creating your inner circles. That is right, multiple inner circles.

> Step #1: Create an inner circle of people who think exactly like you.

> These people think the same thoughts and always agree with you. This inner circle is a critical key to success and will ensure you have the confidence to eventually think differently.

> Step #2: Create an inner circle of people who think exactly opposite of you.

> These are people who will always disagree with what you think is right. These people will be key to expanding your horizons and

thought processes. This may feel counterintuitive at first. However, if you give the process time and invest in the process it will work.

Step #3: Create an inner circle of people who think like you and think different thoughts.

These people usually see things the same way as you do and will agree with your decisions most of the time. However, in some situations, they will challenge you and ensure you have thought of everything before moving forward.

Step #4: Create a Master Inner Circle.

Once you have had some experience with the three inner circles you have already created, create a new, Master Inner Circle. This Master Inner Circle will be made up of one person from each of the other three groups and two new people. The three people you pick from the original groups should be those who match you closely personality wise, be people who can push you when you need to be pushed and be people who excel at your weaknesses. The other two should be people who have achieved a greater level of success than you. This is critical to your success because you always want to surround yourself with people who can push you to get to the next level.

Great job!

You are 1/3rd of the way through!

Now, we will move on to the next method, Record Your Thoughts.

How to Think Differently #3: Record Your Thoughts

Get a hand-held recorder. While you could use your smartphone or tablet for this, it is not recommended. You want to have a common device to record your thoughts at any given time and you want to be able to unplug from the world and still record your thoughts. While you could do things on your phone to ensure you do not get calls and texts, it goes deeper than that. The fact of having the phone in your pocket means your subconscious is still *thinking* about it and does not free up your entire mind to explore all possibilities.

Start off by recording what you feel comfortable recording. It may be only a few words and just enough to jog your memory later on. It may be more complete thoughts, the same as if you were talking to someone. In fact you may record your side of the conversation when you talk to people. For example, say you are talking to Sally and have a thought that you would like to change. Get out your pocket recorder, let Sally know what is going on and record your thoughts. I then recommend turning the recorder off and not recording the reaction of your listener. You do not want to make your listener uncomfortable and you always want your listener to be completely open with you. This may not happen if you record their answers.

Now, we will move on to how to Flip Things Around.

How to Think Differently #4:
Flip Things Around

The next time you have a small decision to make that you have made before without much success, do exactly the opposite of what you think you should do.   Here is a disclaimer: Your goal is to get more business, and not lose business. The goal of this section of the book is to help change your mindset and get more business.   There is no suggestion, endorsement or implication you should do anything illegal, immoral or unethical.   In the end, you are responsible for your actions and for whether or not you chose to take this advice.

This suggestion of starting this process off by doing the complete opposite of what you would have done in the past is because this will open your mind to the possibility of success.   The success rate on this initial shift is around 50%. However, it is a necessary step in the process to improve your results down the road.   Use the results of this decision to make changes in the next decision you need to make. Keep doing this process until you receive the desired results.

For example, say your normal response time to an email is very quick (the same day or even the same hour).   The next few emails that are not critical, try waiting a few days or a week to respond. The rationale behind this change is that a quick response means you are not busy and people want to do business with people who are doing business with other people.

Now, we will move on to how to Try Something New.

How to Think Differently #5:
Try Something New

For you to try something new, you will need to do more than flip things around and more than only doing something differently than you have done in the past. It goes deeper than either of those two things. When clients see what it is, some are scared and others who saw this book before it was published had the desire to turn the page and skip this chapter. If you feel this way, here is a challenge to you to resist the urge and keep reading.

You see, change is hard. Most human beings are built to resist change. This includes the people who say they are ok with change. Mind you, there are some people who are truly ok with change and if you are one of those select few people, wonderful! If you are one of those few, select people, this exercise will be easy for you. If you are like the rest of us, this exercise may feel uncomfortable at first. Stick with it, you will see the results and be glad you did.

Step #1: Determine the thought process you want to change.

Ask yourself this very important question.

What do you want to change?

The recommendation here is to go with the thing that will make the biggest impact in your life. Here is a process to figure it out. If you already feel you know what will make the biggest impact in your life, wonderful!   You can skip to Step #2. Everyone else, read on.

Step #1a: Take a piece of paper or your favorite computer program and make a list of all of the thought processes or actions you want to change.

Step #1b: Put four columns to the right of the list you just made.

Step #1c: Label the columns as follows.

  Column #1: Importance
  Column #2: Personal Impact
  Column #3: Impact to Others
  Column #4: Total

Step #1d: On a scale from 1 to 10, put a rating in each of the columns as follows.

Importance: 1 = Minor Importance;
10 = Very Important
Personal Impact: 1 = Minor Impact;
10 = Major Impact
Impact to Others: 1 = Minor Impact;
10 = Major Impact

Step #1e: Multiply the results of the three columns and put the result in the Total column.

Step #1f: Reorder your list from highest to lowest based on the Total column. The item with the highest total should make the biggest impact on your life.

Step #2: Determine your ideal time length.

You need to determine how long you are going to do this exercise; seven days, fourteen days, thirty days, etc. My clients usually find thirty days is the right amount of time to do this exercise and that they see the best results when trying to change an idea, habit or thought pattern by doing it for thirty consecutive days.

Step #3: During your Ideal Time, do a lot of reflecting.

In this step, thinking is the key. Think about why you were thinking or doing things the old way.   Ask yourself these questions.

Why did you want to do what you were doing?

What was the driver of how you were thinking?

Did it make you feel a certain way?

Did it send vibrations through your body?

Did what you were doing make you think a certain way?

Did you see your mood changing?

Step #4: Once you figure out the answers to the questions in Step #3, figure out what else you can do to give yourself the same positive feeling and thoughts.

Step #5: Once you have the list from Step #4, work through the list and determine which ones are better than what you are currently doing and which ones are worse than what you are currently doing.   Each person determines for themselves what is better and what is worse.

Step #6: Once you have determined which of the actions are better, rank them from 1 to x (x is how many items you have). #1 should be the most impactful and the last one should be the least impactful. Here again, you decide what constitutes impactful to you.

Step #7: Implement the #1 item on your list for your ideal time.

You are almost there! One more to go!

The last method for this book is to Reflect and Plan.

How to Think Differently #6: Reflect and Plan

As you move through the process of thinking differently, a key to your success will be reflecting on your activities of the day to ensure you are making progress and intentionally planning for the next day to ensure your limited energy is being used in the right direction.

When we talked about overcoming the Hidden Barrier to More (_____*) #8: Your Timing is Off, we discussed reflecting and planning with a purpose. In that section, we talked about reflecting and planning to overcome fears. This section describes reflecting and planning in general and how to get the most out of it.

To get the most out of reflecting and planning, you should:

- ✓ Reflect nightly and plan for the next day.
- ✓ Reflect weekly and plan for the upcoming week.
- ✓ Reflect monthly and plan for the upcoming month.
- ✓ Reflect yearly and plan for the next year.

Each timeframe will require a somewhat different reflection method. This is over and above the obvious thing of reflecting for a different amount of time.

Element #1: Daily Reflect and Plan Cycle

Each night, use the time right before you go to bed to reflect on the accomplishments from the day and plan for the next day. This plan should be as detailed as necessary to ensure you will get what you need to get done the following day done. This should include blocking off specific times of the day for specific activities and prioritizing things so that you get the most impactful things done early in the day and leave the items that are less impactful until later in the day.

The initial basis for this daily plan should be taken right from the weekly plan. Because, at the beginning of each week, you decided what would be important to get done that week. Unless things change a great deal, you should stick as close as possible to the plan you created at the beginning of the week.

There is a reason you do this right before you go to bed. Studies show that while you are sleeping your subconscious will think about whatever you were consciously thinking about the last 15 minutes before you went to bed. This will allow you to harness the great power of your subconscious to figure out the challenges of the coming day.

Element #2: Weekly Reflect and Plan Cycle

Every weekend, take some time to review the accomplishments and challenges from the previous week. Unlike the daily reflect and plan cycle, this does not have to be done right before bed. However, it should be done at a time when you will not be disturbed so that you can give this process 100% of your attention. Ask yourself the following questions:

What went well this past week and what did not go so well?

What from the plan did get accomplished?

What from the plan did not get accomplished and why?

What got in the way of accomplishing the things on the plan?

What is left on the list from this week that is no longer important?

The key here is to monitor how things are going on a regular basis to stop things from getting out of hand and stop bad habits from forming.

Element #3: Monthly Reflect and Plan Cycle

At the end of every month, take some time to review the accomplishments and challenges from the previous month. Like the weekly reflect and plan cycle, this does not have to be done right before bed. However, it should be done at a time when you will not be disturbed so that you can give this process 100% of your attention.   Ask yourself the following questions:

What went well this past month and what did not go so well?

What from the plan did get accomplished?

What from the plan did not get accomplished and why?

What got in the way of accomplishing the things on the plan?

What is left on the list from this month that is no longer important?

While these are the same questions as the weekly reflect and plan cycle, you are asking them for a different reason. Because you do not want to have to review everything at a very granular level again, focus on high-level items.   For example, maybe you found out from the weekly reflect and plan cycle that you did not get the updates done to your website like you had planned. Maybe you then found out during the monthly reflect and plan cycle that five out of the six internet-related items you planned on doing during the month did not get done. You may interpret from this finding that you need to hire someone to take care of your internet presence or things will not get done.

Once again, the key here is to monitor how things are going on a regular basis to stop things from getting out of hand and stop bad habits from forming.

Element #4: Yearly Reflect and Plan Cycle

At the end of every year, take some time to review the accomplishments and challenges from the previous year. Like both the weekly reflect and plan cycle and the monthly reflect and plan cycle, this does not have to be done right before bed. However, it should be done at a time when you will not be disturbed so that you can give this process 100% of your attention. Ask yourself the following questions:

What made this a great year?

What should have not been done this past year?

Who should time be invested in over the next year?

Who have I outgrown over this past year?

Who would be good to connect with in the coming year?

What are the goals for the coming year?

What feelings will there be when the goals are achieved?

At a high level, what is required to achieve these goals?

What is the confidence level that these are the right goals?

What is the confidence level these goals will be achieved?

What will it mean when these goals are achieved?

What are the roadblocks to achieving these goals?

At a high-level, what things should be put in place to help with or overcome the roadblocks?

What learning goals are there for the next year?

Is an accountability partner needed? If so, who?

Are there any clients that should be fired? If so, who and why?

The key here is to ask thought-provoking questions.

Do you have some additional questions that help you or someone you know to reflect and plan?

Share them by visiting:

http://TheSecretBlueprintToMore.com/reflect

Conclusion

Remember, this is the start of your journey. The hope is that you were inspired by this book and are now on your own journey to master your mindset, do what is necessary to live the life you deserve and realize that all great changes happen over time. These changes may seem to the outside world as they happened in an instant. The truth is that it is not the first or the last action you take that makes the difference. It is every action in-between and everything you do on a regular basis. These actions create the momentum necessary to make the changes you desire happen and make them last for a lifetime.

On a personal note, I would love to hear from you about the changes in your life and how this book has helped you master your mindset. Throughout the book, there were several websites listed where you can share specific stories and successes. Please also feel free to send your emails to:

TheSecretBlueprintToMore@sangnite.com

Keep on reading for some great bonus material!

Bonus #1: Share Your Experiences

"Sharing knowledge with another is the greatest gift one can give." **Chris M. Sprague**

Share Your Experiences

While reading this book, did you find yourself saying ANY of the following?

> *There are more secrets that have not been covered.*
>
> *There are more keys that have not been revealed.*
>
> *Sharing my experiences would be fun.*

Wonderful! We need to talk about you being one of the select people to be featured in future editions of *The Secret Blueprint to More (_____*)*. The goal of future editions will be to craft books geared towards specific audiences. Future editions will include; *The Secret Blueprint to More (_____*)* for:

- ✓ Leaders
- ✓ Entrepreneurs
- ✓ CEOs
- ✓ Sales Professionals
- ✓ Human Resource Professionals
- ✓ Information Technology Professionals
- ✓ Recruiters

... and the list goes on and on. At a high level, approximately 10 professionals (like you) in each field will be interviewed and you and your experiences will serve as the basis for the book. Once the interview is complete, a complete chapter will be written about you using your experiences as the basis for revealing to other people the keys you used to master your mindset. The book will also include a short biography about you and a section where you can advertise and promote your business. Other program benefits include:

- ✓ You will receive 5 copies of the book where you are featured on the cover with the chance to purchase other copies of the book at a deep discount.
- ✓ You will be featured in all promotions for the book you are in.
- ✓ We take care of all of the writing and publishing tasks.

If you have seen programs like this before, you know they usually cost thousands of dollars. However, here is a special limited-time offer for you. If you are one of the first 20 people to apply and get approved, your enrollment investment (currently $995), will be _waived_!

You read right the first 20 people to apply and get approved will be featured in a book and get a large amount of publicity (teleseminars, webcasts, press releases and much more) for free!

In general, whether it is the first twenty or the participants after that, all participants will be chosen based on a short interview process and on a first-come, first-served basis. This means that for each book, the first ten or so people in each category that apply and are approved get in the book.

For more information and to apply, please visit:

http://TheSecretBlueprintToMore.com/shareyourexperience

Bonus #2: The BE A Success Academy

(The Barrier Elimination and Success Academy)

> *"When you master your mindset, everything is possible." Chris M. Sprague*

The BE A Success Academy: Overview

This is a 3-phase system where you will work with certified mindset, empowerment, business and personal coaching experts to ensure your success.

> Phase 1: Uncover and Eliminate Barriers
> Phase 2: Get Laser Focused
> Phase 3: Epic Success

Phase 1 and Phase 2 will be a mix of intensive one-on-one and group coaching along with teleseminars, webcasts and other special surprises. During Phase 3, you will attend a live event with others in the program where you will spend 2.5 days with your peers and coaches to cement what you learned in Phases 1 and 2 and leave with the rest of the tools you need to be the epic success you were born to be.

In addition to the above, you will have access to private groups on both LinkedIn and Facebook and much, much more. Read on for an overview of each phase.

Phase 1: Uncover and Eliminate Barriers

This phase will focus on eliminating barriers and ensuring you have the mindset to succeed.

What do Donald Trump, Richard Branson, Steve Jobs, Bill Gates and John Maxwell all have in common?

Other than being wildly successful, they all have a different mindset than most people. Whether it is Donald Trump waking up and reading as many newspapers as possible on a daily basis or Richard Branson doing things no one else would dream of doing, each of these people have mastered the art of thinking differently. Now, you can too!

Do you know there is more out there for you?

Do you know you are not living up to your fullest potential?

Do you want more out of life?

Do you want to get there faster than you ever thought possible?

In Phase 1 of the program, we dig down deep to determine your current strengths and weaknesses, understand your past and present, help you put down your baggage and plan your future, give you tools to focus on your strengths and backfill your weaknesses and set up a process where you will successfully reflect and plan on a regular basis.

Phase 2: Get Laser Focused

This phase will ensure you do the things necessary to do the necessary things.

How many times has the following happened to you?

You go to a website, conference or live event, love the speaker or content and then spend between a few dollars and a few thousand dollars on books, DVDs, CDs, programs, etc. that are now gathering dust on your bookshelf.   If you are like many clients, the answer is all the time.

What if you could finally use all of those programs and start making money with them?

What if you could go through all of those programs and decide which ones were right for you?

What if you could make money off of the programs that were not right for you?

In Phase 2 of the program, we work with you to go through your entire library, program by program and see where it fits in with your new mindset. For those programs that are a definite fit, we work with you to come up with a plan of action and ensure you take the steps necessary to complete each program. For those programs that may or may not be a fit for you, we set them aside and keep them for review at a later date. For those programs that are no longer a fit for you, we help you resell them or trade them for programs that will fit your new mindset.

Phase 3: Epic Success

If you are like most people, you want to stand on your own, be independent and be dependent on yourself for your own success. You understand that you need resources and people to turn to when times get tough and do not want to feel like you *always* need someone to help you be successful. You like to determine how and when you get help. You know that *sometimes* you need help to get over a hump or get your momentum restarted and other times, you are fine on your own. That is what sets this program apart.

In Phase 3 of the program, you transition from intensive coaching to relying on yourself and the rest of your peers for most things. You will also be part of a larger community that will be there to support you on your journey. Think of it as a safety net to ensure your success!

For more information and to apply to this exclusive experience, please visit: http://BEASuccessAcademy.org

Notes and Internet References

1: *StrengthsFinder 2.0* by Tom Rath, Gallup Press, 2007, http://www.strengthsfinder.com/home.aspx

2: *StandOut* by Marcus Buckingham, Thomas Nelson, 2011, http://standout.tmbc.com/gui/

3: Let people know about your progress.

Overcoming Barrier #1: Understand and Accept Yourself
http://TheSecretBlueprintToMore.com/accept

Overcoming Barrier #2: Transform Your Thinking
http://TheSecretBlueprintToMore.com/transform

Overcoming Barrier #3: Write Out the Details
http://TheSecretBlueprintToMore.com/write

Overcoming Barrier #5: Focus on the Present
http://TheSecretBlueprintToMore.com/focus

Overcoming Barrier #6: The 5 Project Review
http://TheSecretBlueprintToMore.com/projectreview

Overcoming Barrier #9: Use Passion, Strengths and Commitment

http://TheSecretBlueprintToMore.com/keys

How to Think Differently #6: Reflect and Plan

http://TheSecretBlueprintToMore.com/reflect

4: Great opportunity to share your experiences.

http://TheSecretBlueprintToMore.com/shareyourexperience

5: Eliminate barriers for good and BE A Success.

http://BEASuccessAcademy.org

About the Author:
Chris M. Sprague

Empowering, impressive, passionate, powerful and inspirational are a few words that have been used to describe Chris. As a motivational teacher, coach and mentor, his goal is to inspire and motivate you to master your mindset so you can be the best you can be.

His clients include business owners and entrepreneurs along with individuals and companies in the areas of sales, human resources, relationship marketing, information technology and health & fitness.

His life experience, knowledge, and passion for achievement allow him to create for you a compelling and empowering seminar or retreat and an engaging one-on-one and group coaching environment. Engage with Chris and you will have an event and an experience like no other. He brings passion and energy into the room with enthusiasm for and knowledge of the mind, leadership, effectively connecting with people, body language and other subjects key to helping you break through barriers and achieve your goals.

Combining humor, stories and content to entertain and educate audiences, he will equip you with the tools necessary to master your mindset and drive lasting improvements that create greater success in today's challenging environment. He speaks and listens from the heart and cares at a very deep level about people he connects with which allows him to add value to you that will last a lifetime.

Chris says, "Two of the biggest keys to eliminating barriers and mastering your mindset are to intentionally grow and to be constantly learning. These are things that I live and breathe on a daily basis. Because my mission is to be a river and not a reservoir, working together, you will benefit from my constant and never-ending thirst for knowledge by receiving the latest and greatest tips and techniques along with tried and true methods to enhance your abilities, eliminate barriers and to master your mindset."

Here is what Carla Andrews, President, Signature Living, Inc. (www.signatureliving.com) said about Chris, "Chris M. Sprague is an emerging thinker among the art and science of building successful businesses. He can help you discover the leadership principles needed to help you believe in your ability to reach your potential and goals. As Chris helps you to commit to your long term goals, he knows how to handle difficult and challenging situations and lead you to appreciate the journey as much as the destination. Chris M. Sprague is THE coach, speaker, and teacher for your personal and business needs."

Visit http://chrismsprague.com for more details and samples of Chris' work.

www.ingramcontent.com/pod-product-compliance
Lightning Source LLC
Chambersburg PA
CBHW060612200326
41521CB00007B/750